AN INSPECTOR CALLS

AN ESSAY WRITING GUIDE FOR GCSE

R. P. DAVIS

CONTENTS

FOREWORD

In your GCSE English Literature exam, you will be presented with two questions on J. B. Priestley's *An Inspector Calls*, and you will then be asked to pick just one to answer. Of course, once you've picked the question you prefer, there are many methods you *might* use to tackle it. However, there is one particular technique which, due to its sophistication, most readily allows students to unlock the highest marks: namely, **the thematic method**.

To be clear, this study guide is *not* intended to walk you through the play act-by-act and sequence-by-sequence: there are many great guides out there that do just that. No, this guide, by sifting through a series of mock exam questions, will demonstrate *how* to organise a response thematically and thus write a stellar essay: a skill we believe no other study guide adequately covers!

I have encountered students who have structured their essays all sorts of ways: some who'll write about the play chronologically, others who'll give each character their own paragraph.

The method I'm advocating, on the other hand, involves picking out three to four themes that will allow you to holistically answer the question: these three to four themes will become the three to four content paragraphs of your essay, cushioned between a brief introduction and conclusion. Ideally, these themes will follow from one to the next to create a flowing argument. Within each of these thematic paragraphs, you can then ensure you are jumping through the mark scheme's hoops.

So to break things down further, each thematic paragraph will include various point-scoring components. In each paragraph, you will include quotes from the play (yes, that means you'll have to have some committed to memory!), offer analyses of these quotes, then discuss how the specific language techniques you have identified illustrate the theme you're discussing. And in most every paragraph, you will comment on the era in which the play was written and how that helps to understand the chosen theme.

1) Priestley's profile as rendered in Ivegate Arch, Bradford. Copyright © Tim Green

Don't worry if this all feels daunting. Throughout this guide, I will be illustrating in great detail – by means of examples – how to build an essay of this kind.

The beauty of the thematic approach is that, once you have your themes, you suddenly have a direction and a trajectory, and this makes essay writing a whole lot easier. However, it must also be noted that selecting themes in the first place is something students often find tricky. I have come across many candidates who understand the play inside out; but when they are presented with questions under exam conditions, and the pressure kicks in, they find it tough to break their response down into themes. The fact of the matter is: the process is a *creative* one and the best themes require a bit of imagination.

In this guide, I shall take nine different exam-style questions, and shall put together a plan for each – a plan that illustrates in detail how we will be satisfying the mark scheme's criteria. Please do keep in mind that, when operating under timed conditions, your plans will necessarily be less detailed than those that appear in this volume.

Now, you might be asking whether three or four themes is best. The truth is, you should do whatever you feel most comfortable with: the examiner is looking for an original, creative answer, and not sitting there counting the themes. So if you think you are quick enough to cover four, then great. However, if you would rather do three to make sure you do each theme justice, that's also fine. I sometimes suggest that my student pick four themes, but make the fourth one smaller – sort of like an afterthought, or an observation that turns things on their head. That way, if they feel they won't have time to explore this fourth theme in its own right, they can always give it a quick mention in the conclusion instead.

2) A statue depicting Priestley at his typewriter. Copyright ©
Tim Green

Before I move forward in earnest, I believe it to be worthwhile
to run through the four Assessment Objectives the exam board
want you to cover in your response – if only to demonstrate
how effective the thematic response can be. I would argue that
the first Assessment Objective (AO1) – the one that wants
candidates to 'read, understand and respond to texts' and
which is worth 12 of the total 30 marks up for grabs – will be
wholly satisfied by selecting strong themes, then fleshing them
out with quotes. Indeed, when it comes to identifying the top-
scoring candidates for AO1, the mark scheme explicitly tells
examiners to look for a 'critical, exploratory, conceptualised
response' that makes 'judicious use of precise references' – the
word 'concept' is a synonym of theme, and 'judicious references' simply refers to quotes that appropriately support the
theme you've chosen.

The second Assessment Objective (AO2) – which is also responsible for 12 marks – asks students to 'analyse the language, form and structure used by a writer to create meanings and effects, using relevant subject terminology where appropriate.' As noted, you will already be quoting from the play as you back up your themes, and it is a natural progression to then analyse the language techniques used. In fact, this is far more effective than simply observing language techniques (metaphor here, alliteration there), because by discussing how the language techniques relate to and shape the theme, you will also be demonstrating how the writer 'create[s] meanings and effects.'

Now, in my experience, language analysis is the most important element of AO2 – perhaps 8 of the 12 marks will go towards language analysis. You will also notice, however, that AO2 asks students to comment on 'form and structure.' Again, the thematic approach has your back – because though simply jamming in a point on form or structure will feel jarring, when you bring these points up while discussing a theme, as a means to further a thematic argument, you will again organically be discussing the way it 'create[s] meanings and effects.'

AO3 requires you to 'show understanding of the relationships between texts and the contexts in which they were written' and is responsible for a more modest 6 marks in total. These are easy enough to weave into a thematic argument; indeed, the theme gives the student a chance to bring up context in a relevant and fitting way. After all, you don't want it to look like you've just shoehorned a contextual factoid into the mix.

Finally, you have AO4 – known also as "spelling and grammar." There are four marks up for grabs here. Truth be told, this guide is not geared towards AO4. My advice? Make sure you are reading plenty of books and articles, because the more you read, the better your spelling and grammar will be. Also, before the exam, perhaps make a list of words you struggle to spell but often find yourself using in essays, and commit them to memory.

3) A photo of the *Titanic* in Southhampton in April 1912, prior to its disastrous maiden voyage. Birling's comments about the *Titanic* are key to understanding his character.

My hope is that this book, by demonstrating how to select relevant themes, will help you feel more confident in doing so yourself. I believe it is also worth mentioning that the themes I have picked out are by no means definitive. Asked the very same question, someone else may pick out different themes, and write an answer that is just as good (if not better!). Obviously the exam is not likely to be fun – my memory of them is pretty much the exact opposite. But still, this is one of the very few chances that you will get at GCSE level to actually be creative. And to my mind at least, that was always more enjoyable – if *enjoyable* is the right word – than simply demonstrating that I had memorised loads of facts.

ESSAY PLAN ONE

HOW DOES PRIESTLEY EXPLORE RESPONSIBILITY IN AN INSPECTOR CALLS?

INTRODUCTION

I often suggest kicking off the introduction with a piece of historical or literary context, because this ensures you are scoring AO3 marks (marks that too often get neglected!) right off the bat. It's then a good idea to quickly touch on the themes you are planning to discuss, since this will alert the examiner to the fact that AO1 is also front and centre in your mind.

"Given that in the wake of WW2 the world found itself cleaved between two competing ideologies – an Anglo-American capitalism and Russian style communism – it is unsurprising that Priestley's 1945 play found itself preoccupied with these duelling ideologies.[1] Indeed, a key discrepancy between these ideologies comes under particular scrutiny: their conceptions of social responsibility. If Birling is the voice of the self-interested capitalist who abrogates all social responsibilities, Goole is Priestley's mouthpiece for a socialist dogma that insists social responsibilities be acknowledged: a dogma that sways the younger Birlings yet not the older contingent.[2]"

Theme/Paragraph One: Priestley explores responsibility at the societal level: Birling is the voice of a capitalist *laissez-faire* attitude towards social responsibility, whereas Goole backs a socialist model of heightened responsibility.[3] By casting Goole as the protagonist, and Birling as antagonist, the play tacitly suggests the socialist model is morally superior.

- In the play's opening act, Priestley has Birling sing the praises of the capitalist mentality of minimal social responsibility: in an after-dinner speech, Birling asserts that 'a man has to make his own way – has to look after himself,' and dismisses the idea that 'everybody has to look after everybody else' as 'nonsense.' Birling's vitriol for the socialist model is perhaps best conveyed in a simile likening it to 'bees in a hive' – an image which, by equating the mindset of socialists to that of insects, suggests it to be intellectually regressive and dehumanising. However, Priestley seeks to subvert Birling's attitude from the off. Exploiting the fact that the play is set in 1912, Priestley places comments steeped in dramatic irony in Birling's mouth: Birling dismisses the likelihood of war ('the Germans don't want war') and pronounces the Titanic 'unsinkable.'[4] The self-evident foolishness of these comments immediately throws his entire worldview into question. [*AO1 for advancing the argument with a judiciously selected quote; AO2 for the close analysis of the language; AO3 for placing the text in historical context*].

- Of course, Priestley deconstructs Birling's worldview more emphatically through the character of Goole. The timing of Goole's arrival (almost immediately after Birling's pronouncements) instantly hint that he will offer a counterpoint, and the mere fact he bothers chastising Birling for firing unionised workers, or Sheila for having a shop attendant sacked, points to his socialist bona fides: these are not legal transgressions an inspector would ordinarily follow up, but rather social ones.[5] However, the clearest articulation of his ideology of heightened social responsibility comes in the staccato sentences just prior to his departure in Act 3: 'We are members of one body. We are responsible for each other.' [*AO1 for advancing the argument with a judiciously selected quote; AO2 for discussing how form and structure shapes meaning*].

- The arc and staging of the story – in which the unflappable Goole, who is repeatedly described as 'taking charge,' exposes Birling's blustering hypocrisies – ensures that Goole's view on social responsibility, the one that the socialist-minded Priestley in fact favoured, is the one the audience is encouraged to favour, too. [*AO1 for advancing the argument with a judiciously selected quote*].

Theme/Paragraph Two: As the play unfolds, Goole is able to instil a sense of responsibility in

the Birling children, yet fails to achieve the same with their parents. The play is an exploration of the degree to which people might be awakened to the ideology of social responsibility.

- As Goole turns his attentions to Sheila later in Act 1, and dredges up the occasion she had a woman (supposedly Eva Smith) sacked from her job at a clothing store, Sheila proves credulous to Goole's idea that this incident, while perhaps not a legal transgression, had contributed to that girl's suicide. Goole explicitly asserts that Sheila is 'partly to blame,' and Sheila internalises the notion: by the start of Act 2 (a heart-beat later in the play's structure), Sheila is keenly shouldering the responsibility: 'I know I'm to blame – and I'm desperately sorry.' Even when Gerald, in Act 3, discovers that Goole was in fact *not* on the police force and there had been no woman in the infirmary, Sheila maintains a sense that they still ought to be shouldering responsibility: her sardonic response to her parents' blame dodging – 'So there's nothing to be sorry for, nothing to learn' – makes clear she thinks the exact opposite.[6] [*AO1 for advancing the argument with a judiciously selected quote; AO2 for the close analysis of the language and for discussing how structure shapes meaning*].

- Although more reluctant to face responsibility in the first place (as symbolised by his fleeing the household in Act 2), Eric also eventually proves amenable to Goole's philosophy of responsibility taking (as symbolised by his voluntary return). Of course, in many respects Eric's transgressions are heftier and more legally perilous – he stole, and potentially committed rape – and thus the onus on him to shoulder responsibility is surely greater. Nevertheless, he does indeed do so, echoing Sheila's sentiments in the play's final sequences. [*AO2 for discussing how structure shapes meaning*].

- However, whereas the Birling children internalise the concept – so much so that Sheila starts advocating for this worldview almost as vehemently as Goole – Priestley presents the older Birlings as so repulsed by the idea of social responsibility that, even when faced with their historical acts of cruelty, they refuse to budge: as Mrs Birling puts it near the end of Act 3, 'I have done no more than my duty.' [*AO1 for advancing the argument with a judiciously selected quote*].

Theme/Paragraph Three: Priestley's play explores the difference between taking responsibility and being held responsible. Although the older Birlings may refuse to take responsibility, Priestley explores how all of the Birlings, plus Gerald, are *held* responsible through Goole's interrogations.

- Given that submitting to Goole's interrogations might be considered a kind of punishment in its own right, the persistent questioning each of the dinner attendees face ensures that, even if the character in question refuses to *take* responsibility, they are still *held* responsible. Often it is Priestley's stage directions that best reveal the distress the characters are undergoing as they take their turn under Goole's

spotlight. Even the stubborn Birling and Mrs Birling
are variously described as behaving 'angrily,' 'bitterly'
or 'annoyed' as they weather Goole's interrogations.
Gerald occupies a more equivocal position than the
duelling Birling generations: he is contrite, yet does
not become an evangelical adherent of Goole's
mentality.[7] Nevertheless, he too is held responsible by
Goole, and meets with a very real punishment: losing
his fiancée. [*AO1 for advancing the argument with a
judiciously selected quote; AO2 for the close analysis
of the language*].

- Although the crimes in question are of course not
  analogous, this notion of holding individuals
  responsible – including those who may refuse to
  acknowledge their responsibility – was particularly
  pertinent in the year the play was released.[8] After all,
  four months after the play premiered in July 1945,
  the Nuremberg Trials got underway: trials specifically
  designed to prosecute the key players in the Nazi
  regime, including the unrepentant among them. [*AO3
  for placing the text in historical context*].

- However, it is not just Goole that holds the Birlings to
  account, but the fictional universe in which they exist,
  too. In what Priestley surely wishes the audience to
  construe as a supernatural twist, the Birlings and
  Gerald, after satisfying themselves that at least a
  portion of the night's proceedings had been a hoax,
  receive a call informing them that a girl had just
  committed suicide and that officers are *en route* to
  quiz them.[9] This suggests that their collective
  punishment is about to recommence – indeed, given
  Birling's 'panic-stricken' face, one assumes it already

has. [*AO1 for advancing the argument with a judiciously selected quote*].

- While it has previously been noted that the Birling parents are unrepentant, it is perhaps worth noting that the final stage direction describes all the Birlings and Gerald as staring 'guiltily,' raising the possibility that this final turn of events might have finally forced the older Birlings to acknowledge some responsibility. [*AO1 for advancing the argument with a judiciously selected quote*].

Conclusion

We have a very meaty essay here, so I don't think a standalone fourth theme is necessary – and yet I do have one last idea up my sleeve: namely, that Priestley also asks the audience to consider the extent of their own responsibility. As a result, I have slipped this argument into the conclusion, thereby ensuring that I go out with a bang!

"The idea of responsibility is inseparable from Priestley's play, and bleeds into its every nook and cranny. One might even reflect how Priestley subtly uses his play to explore responsibility on the audience's part as well. Given Goole's systematic grilling of everyone in the room, the audience might be left with the uncomfortable feeling that they might also come under scrutiny themselves at any moment. This dynamic cunningly invites the audience to consider (and, where appropriate, take responsibility for) their own complicity in capitalism's excesses, too."

4) A statue of Priestley in his hometown of Bradford, UK. Copyright © Tim Green

ESSAY PLAN TWO

HOW FAR DOES PRIESTLEY PRESENT ERIC AS AN
HONEST CHARACTER IN AN INSPECTOR CALLS?

INTRODUCTION

Again, you'll notice that I'm kicking the essay off with a bid for
those AO3 marks – this time, by trying to place the text in its
literary context and discussing the prevalence of confession in
twentieth century literature. I then pivot to the themes in *An
Inspector Calls* I'm intending to cover, thus alerting the examiner to the AO1 ideas I have in mind.

"The twentieth century was punctuated by seminal
works that centred on confessions – be it T.S. Eliot's
'The Love Song of J Alfred Prufrock,' (1915) or
Vladimir Nabokov's *Lolita* (1955).[1] Priestley's 1945
play, *An Inspector Calls,* also fraternises with the
concept of confession, as the probing Goole coaxes
each of the Birlings, and Gerald, to reveal the skeletons
in their closets. While Eric appears to embody
dishonesty in his behaviour prior to the action that

unfolds on stage, he *does* come clean in the play's third act. However, it could be argued that his confession does not point to honesty in his character – rather, that he has merely been forced to make a clean breast as a result of Goole's intervention."

Theme / Paragraph One: Not only does it come out that Eric has committed a number of historical transgressions that exemplify dishonesty – chief among them the appropriation of money from his father's business – but, doubling up on his dishonesty, he also worked to conceal these actions.[2]

- If we wish to judge Eric holistically, it is imperative to look at his historical behaviour, which seems to exemplify dishonesty. The key event that speaks to his dishonesty is his stealing money from his father – 'fifty pounds all told,' as Eric puts it. Indeed, the mechanism Eric used to steal this money explicitly involved deceiving his father's clients: he 'gave the firm's receipts and then kept the money,' as Birling rightly deduces. What is striking, too, is that even as Eric confesses this misdemeanour, he is unable to be honest with himself regarding the nature of the crime: when Goole bluntly asks him whether he stole ('you stole money?'), Eric rebuffs Goole's choice of words: 'Not really.' [*AO1 for advancing the argument with a judiciously selected quote; AO2 for the close analysis of the language*].
- If Eric's past behaviour indicates a capacity for dishonesty, then so too does his decision to then

conceal his sordid pattern of behaviour from his family. Of course, Eric had concealed his entire liaison with Eva Smith/Daisy Renton from his family; but he had also attempted to conceal plenty more – for instance, his drinking habit, which Mrs Birling was utterly unaware of. Indeed, she is described as 'staggered' when she hears it from Sheila. [*AO1 for advancing the argument with a judiciously selected quote*].

Theme/Paragraph Two: Although Eric exhibited extreme dishonesty with his past behaviour, he *does* embrace honesty when he returns to the Birling household.

- The fact that Eric makes a deliberate decision to opt for honesty is perhaps best exemplified by the staging. When Eric flees the house in Act 2, it appears as though he has decided to double down on his tactic of concealment. Yet his return at the end of Act 2 acts as to physically telegraph his decision to come clean. Indeed, as the curtain comes up on Act 3, the stagecraft mirrors Eric's imminent honesty: a metaphorical curtain is coming up on his previously concealed transgressions. Eric's body language prior to his big confession also indicates a marked change towards greater honesty: the stage direction notes that his 'whole manner' when pouring himself a drink 'shows his familiarity with quick heavy drinking.' He is no longer dissembling to conceal his vice.[3] [*AO1 for advancing the argument with a judiciously selected quote; AO2 for discussing how structure shapes meaning*].

- Of course, immediately after taking this drink, Eric proceeds to lay his cards on the table, and admits to potentially raping Eva Smith/Daisy Renton while under the influence, as well as getting her pregnant and stealing from his father. It is true, as mentioned earlier, that he at times appears to deceive himself during his confession; however, by the time he is finished confessing, he seems not only willing to be candid with himself – 'I did what I did,' he concedes tautologically – but also unwilling to engage in Birling's fresh plan to implement a cover-up to avoid a 'public scandal.'[4] [*AO1 for advancing the argument with a judiciously selected quote; AO2 for the close analysis of the language*].

- It is also worth noting that once Eric confesses, he exhibits no regret in having done so. This suggests that truth-telling is *not* at odds with his personality, whereas it appears to be for his parents, who bemoan having allowed any of the truths to come out.

Theme/Paragraph Three: However, to what extent is the honesty foisted on him by Goole? It could even be argued that he should be due even less credit, since the facts are already out by the time he confesses: he has no choice but to face the music.

- Eric's opening words at the start of Act 3 are telling: 'You know, don't you?' Implicit is a sense of resignation: an understanding that, since the facts are already out, he has no choice but to confess, a sentiment that suggests that his ensuing transparency is not borne from an intrinsic honesty, but from entrapment. Not only does this communicate a latent reluctance – if they had not already known, Eric may well have decided to keep mum – but it also points to the fact that, in many ways, Eric's ensuing honesty is moot; after all, the others already know ('Yes, we know,' the Inspector replies.).[5] [*AO1 for advancing the argument with a judiciously selected quote*].

- Indeed, Eric's opprobrium towards Sheila when hearing she had revealed his drinking habit speaks volumes: '*You* told her. Why, you little sneak!'[6] The italicised '*You*' combined with the exclamation mark of course underscore his frustration at being unmasked; but the word 'sneak' is particularly interesting, for it paradoxically suggests that divulging truths is in fact a duplicitous and "sneaky" thing to do. [*AO1 for advancing the argument with a judiciously selected quote*].

- Therefore, given that honesty appears ultimately to be foisted on Eric, it may be reasonable to temper the credit granted to him for his confession: it seems the result *not* of an honest strain in his personality, but of a capitulation to circumstance.[7]

Theme/Paragraph Four: There is a kind of social honesty about Eric from the start that is exemplified by his sarcastic comments. In a sense, he is more honest with his family members about their faults than any other character besides Goole.

- It should be noted that prior to Goole's arrival, Eric, by means of sarcastic asides and interjections, is surprisingly honest with the other members of the cast about their flaws and foibles. In response to Sheila insult ('you're squiffy'), for example, Eric makes a sly and leading remark: 'If you think that's the best she can do–.' Although Eric leaves the crux of the sentence unspoken – indeed, the dash at the end draws this to our attention – the comment, in spite of the self-censorship, still makes amply clear that Sheila is not the straight-laced individual she may initially seem. Another case in point arises when Birling announces his intention to engage in 'speech-making,' to which Eric replies: 'Well, don't do any.' Eric is of course gently indicating to his father that he considers him socially domineering. Tellingly, the stage direction suggests that the comment should be said 'not too rudely,' which of course suggests an undercurrent of rudeness still remains. In a social world where manners often require individuals to dissemble, his flirtation with rudeness is a marker of authenticity and honesty. [*AO1 for advancing the argument with a judiciously selected quote; AO2 for the close analysis of the language and for discussing how form shapes meaning*].

- If Eric is slyly honest with the other *dramatis personae* prior to Goole's arrival and interrogations, he is far more blunt in the wake of Goole's departure.[8] For instance, he tells his father candidly that 'he is not the kind of father a chap could go to when he's in trouble' – a damningly honest indictment of his father's lack of empathy. [*AO1 for advancing the argument with a judiciously selected quote*].

Conclusion

The essay plan we've got here is strong on AO1 and AO2, but is falling short on historical context. As a result, I've made the decision to put historical context front and centre of my conclusion to ensure I'm picking up the marks.

"The war years that immediately preceded the premiere of *An Inspector Calls* were marked by persistent deception between world powers – be it America's Ghost Army of inflatable tanks that deployed in Europe in 1944, or Germany's own attempts to conceal its atrocities from the allied powers. In a world where deceptions were deliberate, and were to be sustained right up until the point they could be sustained no longer, Eric seems to fit right in. Yet while Eric in many ways seems to embody a mentality of deception, he does have a knack for speaking truth to those around him."

5) A photo from February 2011 of the A. D. Players'
production of *An Inspector Calls* at *The George*. Eric can be
seen in the background, watching on sardonically as Birling
delivers his monologue. Copyright © Orlando Arriaga

ESSAY PLAN THREE

HOW FAR DOES PRIESTLEY PRESENT GERALD AS CAPABLE OF CHANGE?

Introduction

On this occasion, the historical context I'm using to start the essay (and to score early AO3 marks) is in fact a film. As long as it's relevant, invoking a film as opposed to another work of literature is completely valid. In fact, *The Third Man* is a great watch if you are into detective films, and you can watch it while legitimately claiming that you are revising for your exams.

"Against the backdrop of seismic geopolitical change, the fiction of the mid to late 1940s frequently dealt with characters undergoing seismic shifts in personality: Carol Reed's film *The Third Man* (1949), for example, features the ruthless Harry Lime, a criminal almost unrecognisable to his childhood friend. Priestley's play also dramatises tectonic shifts in personality: the Birling children transform in real time as they grapple with their historic cruelties. Gerald's journey, however, seems more equivocal. Yet while he may experience less of an on-stage moral awakening, he does demonstrate a capacity for change, both in his historical behaviour and elsewhere."

Theme/Paragraph One: Although the most seismic character changes in the play appear to be moral ones (for instance, the moral awakening exhibited by Sheila), Gerald enacts a different type of change: he proves capable of bucking distress and reclaiming calm.

- One of the most striking aspects of Gerald's character is his capacity to bring about a change in his own mental state. Although other characters prove perhaps more thrown by Goole's forced transparency, Gerald still becomes plenty distressed when Goole starts dredging up his affair with Daisy Renton. Near the end of Act 1 – when Goole briefly leaves the room, and Sheila, prior to Goole explicitly spelling it out, deduces Gerald's affair – Gerald betrays his flustered nerves with his exhortation to Sheila to keep silent: 'So – for God's sake – don't say anything to the Inspector.' Not only does invoking God ('for God's sake') and the litany of dashes hint to his frayed nerves, but so too does the structural choice of placing the comment at the end of the act, which seems to imbue the comment with even greater urgency. [*AO1 for advancing the argument with a judiciously selected quote; AO2 for the close analysis of the language and for discussing how structure and form shapes meaning*].

- If his words alone were not enough to indicate his frayed nerves, the stage directions as he elaborates on the affair in Act 2 make it abundantly clear: he talks 'bitterly' at one point and uncharacteristically cuts Mrs Birling off 'rather impatiently' at another. [*AO1 for advancing the argument with a judiciously selected quote*].

- However, when Gerald returns in Act 3, he reappears a changed man. Granted, he has become privy to a fresh revelation; yet, by merely stepping outside and 'think[ing] things out,' he proves capable of bringing about a change in his mental state. Of course, given the final twist, we are not supposed to construe this type of change as morally worthwhile or useful – on the contrary, it proves futile. Nevertheless, it still unequivocally casts Gerald as a character capable of change. [*AO1 for advancing the argument with a judiciously selected quote*].

Theme/Paragraph Two: Although Gerald undergoes a sharp change in temperament during the course of the play, he does not seem to undergo the same kind of moral awakening as Eric and Sheila: he is far more aligned with the unrepentant older Birling contingent.

- In the third act, just before the final twist, there is a vast discrepancy between the older and younger Birlings. Whereas Eric and Sheila (indeed, especially

Sheila) have internalised Goole's teachings regarding social responsibility – Eric's assertion that 'he was our inspector all right' crystallising the seriousness with which he and Sheila took Goole's messages – the older Birlings remain stubbornly unchanged by the experience: 'there's every excuse for what both your mother and I did.' Gerald, however, bucks the generational trends, for he in fact appears to align more closely with the older Birlings: when Birling asserts that 'it makes *all* the difference' whether Goole was a fraud – the implication of the comment being that he is more concerned about the fallout than the morality of his actions – Gerald wholeheartedly agrees. [*AO1 for advancing the argument with a judiciously selected quote; AO2 for the close analysis of the language*].

- Gerald lack of moral awakening or change is made to seem all the more stark in comparison to the seismic nature of Sheila's change. Sheila, now worlds away from the petty individual who had had a shop assistant fired, is keen to point out that, even if Goole was a charlatan and there had been no suicide, their transgressions had still taken place: 'Everything we said had happened really had happened.'[1] Gerald, however, has learned no such lesson: 'Everything's all right now, Sheila.' [*AO1 for advancing the argument with a judiciously selected quote; AO2 for the close analysis of the language*].

Theme/Paragraph Three: Not only might it be argued that Gerald's sins were less heinous than the Birlings', thereby giving him less manoeuvre for positive change, but it could also be argued

that, by breaking off his affair with Renton, Gerald demonstrated a capacity for moral growth and change.

- Although it is true that Sheila and Eric experience a more radical on-stage moral transformation than Gerald, it might be argued that their sins were more egregious, and thus there was more to motivate them to change – and this perhaps makes a like-for-like comparison between the younger Birlings and Gerald less instructive.[2] Further, there was arguably more room for Eric and Sheila to change in the first place; after all, Gerald was in fact kind to Daisy: he supported her financially and 'at least had some affection for her and made her happy for a time,' as Goole notes. [*AO1 for advancing the argument with a judiciously selected quote*].

- It may also be argued that Gerald's central moral transgression was in fact against Sheila – he was cheating on her – and this was something he gave up by his own volition: he admits that he adored Renton's attention 'for a time,' but the temporal nature of that comment indicates that he was eventually able to overcome his vanity and break things off; and, sure enough, that is precisely what he did: 'I broke it off definitely.' If one is to construe this as an instance of moral growth and maturity, it indicates that Gerald *does* possess a capacity for change – it was simply a change that took place prior to the night of Goole's visit. [*AO1 for advancing the argument with a judiciously selected quote; AO2 for the close analysis of the language*].

- In fact, that Gerald was able to make this change

without Goole's intervention may even indicate that he has a more innate capacity for change than the other Birlings.

Theme/Paragraph Four: Gerald – particularly at the start of the play – shows himself as capable of changing the persona he projects in his social interactions: he is demonstrative to Sheila, diplomatic with Eric, and deferential to Birling.

- Looking beyond the kind of wholesale personality changes that make the play memorable, Gerald demonstrates he is capable of change in a different sense: namely, he is capable of tailoring and shifting his persona to suit the person to whom he is conversing. This is particularly evident in the opening act: at some points (specifically, when addressing Sheila) he is the ardent suitor ('[I] hope I can make you as happy as you deserve to be'); at others, he is the jocular brother-in-law-to-be ('Unless Eric's been up to something', he jokes when Goole is first reported to be at the door); and, at still others, he is the deferential prospective son-in-law: 'I believe you're right, sir' is his response to Birling's pronouncements. [*AO1 for advancing the argument with a judiciously selected quote; AO2 for the close analysis of the language*].
- Gerald thus proves himself capable of changing his persona to suit his interlocutor – indeed, he proves far more able to do so than the Birlings, all of whom seem to have a more uniform way of dealing with the other *dramatis personae*.[3]

Conclusion

In July 1945, the same month in which *An Inspector Calls* premiered, the United Kingdom itself underwent a kind of shift in personality: Clement Atlee's left-wing Labour party beat Winston Churchill's incumbent Conservatives in a landslide. Whereas Sheila makes a similar shift towards a more left-wing mentality of greater social responsibility, Gerald does not undergo such a change while on stage, although he demonstrates not only a charitable side in his treatment of Renton, but also a capacity for change in giving her up. Curiously, the airing of this historical baggage changes Gerald in yet another way: that is, in the way Sheila perceives him. As she states after the revelation: 'You and I aren't the same people who sat down to dinner.'

6) Another photo from the A. D. Players' performance. This time, the shot shows Gerald (right) in tense conversation with Inspector Goole (left). Copyright © Orlando Arriaga

ESSAY PLAN FOUR

HOW FAR DOES PRIESTLEY PRESENT MR BIRLING AS MOTIVATED BY SOCIAL STANDING?

Introduction

"Anxieties about class and social standing saturated the artistic output of the first half of the twentieth century. Charlie Chaplin's hugely popular silent films were a case in point: *City Lights* (1931), for instance, charts the desperate attempts of Chaplin's tramp, the arch symbol of poverty, to affect a higher social status so he might have a chance at wooing a blind woman. If Chaplin's focus was on an individual at the bottom of the social food chain, Priestley's in *An Inspector Calls* is on those at the top. The industrialist Mr Birling is undoubtedly motivated by social standing – both his own and his family's – for he identifies it as a means to brokering power. Yet as an avatar for capitalism, Birling is animated greatly by the profit motive, too."

Theme/Paragraph One: Birling is clearly preoccupied with his own social standing. However, while he is certainly motivated by the prospect of boosting his own social standing, it is clear there are underpinning motivations at play: pride, power, and freedom from accountability.

- That Birling is hungry to boost his personal social standing is best exemplified by his preoccupation with securing a knighthood. The first time he mentions it, he does so with a contrived nonchalance intended to convey indifference: he tells Gerald he stands to gain 'just a knighthood, of course' – 'just' casting it as a mere triviality, and 'of course' that it is the least he expects.[1] However, this seeming indifference is gently undercut when, in response to Gerald's congratulations, Birling lets slip a glimmer of anxiety as to whether he has done enough to secure it: he is eager not to jinx it ('it's a bit too early for [congratulations]'), and he feels compelled to rehash his credentials: 'I was Lord Mayor... a sound useful party man.' If a knighthood embodies social elevation, then the degree to which Birling covets it clearly communicates his motivation to boost his social standing. [*AO1 for advancing the argument with a judiciously selected quote; AO2 for the close analysis of the language*].
- It is clear, however, that a heightened social standing is not an end in itself. Rather, Birling sees it as a means to gain power and insulate himself from accountability. This is best demonstrated in his interactions with Goole. Goole's (purported)

association with the law affords him power. As such, the fact Birling quickly finds opportunity to telegraph his social standing following Goole's arrival – 'I was an alderman for a year – and Lord Mayor' – clearly represents an attempt to use his social standing to neutralise Goole's power and assert his own. [*AO1 for advancing the argument with a judiciously selected quote*].

- If Birling's hunger to boost his social standing is tied to power, it is connected also to his sense of pride. The topic of the knighthood arises in the first place, after all, as a result of Birling's anxiety that Gerald's upper-class mother may feel as if Gerald 'might have done better for [himself] socially' than marrying into Birling's family. [*AO1 for advancing the argument with a judiciously selected quote*].

Theme/Paragraph Two: Beyond his own social standing, Birling is also deeply motivated about maintaining, and indeed boosting, his children's social standing. However, this is ultimately because a blow to his children's social standing will impinge on his own.

- In Act 3, after the revelations concerning Eric have come to light, it is immediately clear that Birling is deeply anxious about how these revelations might impact on Eric's public image: he speaks urgently about the need to 'cover up' Eric's theft; and he agonises repeatedly about the prospect of a 'public scandal.' The word 'public' is operative: Birling does not seem to care all that much about the existence of the scandal per se, but only how it might play out in the public domain. [*AO1 for advancing the argument with a judiciously selected quote; AO2 for the close analysis of the language*].

- Yet not only does Birling prove interested in mitigating potential damage done to Eric's reputation, but he proves interested also in boosting Sheila's social standing. Indeed, one of his final lines in the play is to tell Sheila that she had 'better ask Gerald for that ring.' Encoded in this suggestion is the idea that Sheila, as a result of a measly affair, would be foolish to forgo the chance to marry her social superior. [*AO1 for advancing the argument with a judiciously selected quote; AO2 for the close analysis of the language*].

- However, while it is plain that Birling is highly motivated by his desire to maintain his children's social standing, this is ultimately because he understands that their social standings directly impact his own. When discussing the prospect of Eric's transgressions going public, Birling makes clear his chief fear is that it will endanger his potential knighthood: 'I was almost certain for a knighthood in the next Honours List.' [*AO1 for advancing the argument with a judiciously selected quote*].

Theme/Paragraph Three: Birling's sheer lack of interest in the woman at the heart of the scandal that is threatening to subvert both Eric and his own social standing further emphasises the degree to which social standing is Birling's priority.

- Goole's parting speech exhorts the Birling family to

keep the purported suicide victim at the front and centre of their minds: 'One Eva Smith has gone – but there are millions and millions and millions of Eva Smiths and John Smiths still left with us.' However, once Goole departs (yet before Gerald points out the potential holes in Goole's narrative), Birling's focus – as mentioned above – is almost exclusively on the potential for a public scandal, *not* the girl he believes to have killed herself. The structural choice of having Birling so utterly unconcerned about the young woman after Goole's heartfelt speech adds further emphasis to the degree to which social standing – as opposed to empathy or morality – is his priority. [*AO1 for advancing the argument with a judiciously selected quote; AO2 for discussing how structure shapes meaning*].

- The most Birling can muster regarding the dead Eva Smith/Daisy Renton – the woman he has been led to believe (on top of everything else) had been carrying his unborn grandchild – is the begrudging concession that 'it turned out unfortunately.' The word 'it,' insofar as it refers to the woman in question, is a distillation of Birling's dehumanising indifference – she is a mere thing to Birling – and this indifference further underscores how greatly social standing motivates him in comparison. [*AO1 for advancing the argument with a judiciously selected quote; AO2 for the close analysis of the language*].

Theme/Paragraph Four: Perhaps the only potentially distinct motivation from social standing is the accumulation of capital; yet even this is ultimately less of a concern that social standing

- If there is another significant motivating factor in Birling's life, it is the profit motive. That this is an animating force for Birling is communicated in the play's opening act, when he talks excitedly at the prospect of Gerald and Sheila's marriage allowing him to work together with his business competitor, Croft Limited, 'for lower costs and higher prices.' Not only is the 'lower costs' and 'higher prices' phraseology a distillation of the capitalist motive, but the fact he touts this as a concern in his opening speech lends it structural emphasis: this is front and centre of his mind. [*AO1 for advancing the argument with a judiciously selected quote; AO2 for the close analysis of the language and for discussing how structure shapes meaning*].

- Not only is Birling motivated by 'the interests of capital,' but he is motivated too by the imperative to spread a capitalist ideology; after all, he is interrupting his daughter's engagement party in order to discuss the virtues of capitalism.

- In many senses, however, the accumulation of capital might ultimately be deemed a path to an increased social standing. It is telling that near the end of the play, Birling seems to try and offer Goole money in order to protect his and Eric's public reputation: 'Look, Inspector – I'd give thousands – yes, thousands.' The form and patter of his speech – the repetition of 'thousands,' the breathless dashes – gives a sense of bartering: cash in exchange for social standing. [*AO1 for advancing the argument with a judiciously selected quote; AO2 for the close analysis of the language and for discussing how form shapes meaning*].

Conclusion

"Given Priestley's own disdain for the trappings of social status – two decades after his play premiered, Priestley went on to reject the offer of a knighthood – it is perhaps unsurprising that the arch capitalist Birling, Priestley's antagonist, is portrayed as hugely motivated by the prospect of enhancing his social standing. In a sense, to divine Birling's motives, one is best off parsing Priestley's own; after all, Birling's unsavoury behaviour ultimately comes down to Priestley's own motivation to put forward an ideological argument – to advance a socialist worldview that seeks to expose the excesses and vanity Priestley felt the capitalist milieu encouraged."[2]

7) The A. D. Players again. This shot depicts Birling (left) in conversation with his wife, Mrs Birling. Copyright © Orlando Arriaga

ESSAY PLAN FIVE

EXPLORE HOW PRIESTLEY USES SETTING IN AN INSPECTOR CALLS.

INTRODUCTION

"In the wake of WW2, theatre became increasingly spare and temporally focused: the likes of Samuel Beckett's *Waiting for Godot* (1953), for instance, is set over just a few hours and uses but one location: a tree on a barren plain. While Priestley's stage is somewhat busier than Beckett's, Priestley similarly uses just one location and focuses his action over a short time period. In a sense, this reclaiming of the Aristotelian Unities is a tactic Priestley uses not only to heighten drama, but also to draw attention to the detective genre in which he is operating.[1] Yet setting for Priestley is more versatile still: a tool for exploring class tensions, as well as those between the private and public spheres."

Theme/Paragraph One: By having all the on-stage

action take place in one location, and in a tight period of time, Priestley is able to generate tension, excitement, and a sense of entrapment.

- For all the lengthy stage directions that preface Priestley's play, the key takeaway is that all the action is taking place in 'the dining-room of [the Birlings'] fairly large suburban house.' Although characters leave the room, and occasionally the house, this room and the stage remain synonymous throughout the play, persisting as the focal point at all times.[2] There is, moreover, a strange magnetism to the room that seems to draw people back to it: Gerald leaves the house in Act 2, yet returns in Act 3, while Eric leaves unannounced shortly after Gerald – 'We hear the door slam again' – only to return at the close of Act 2. The only major character who leaves with seemingly no intention of returning is Goole; even then, however, the sense of a return remains with the final announcement that 'a police inspector is on his way here.' The word 'here,' which is given particular structural emphasis as a result of appearing in the play's final line, not only emphasises the centripetal nature of the room, but also reminds the audience bearing witness that, for them, 'here' has been everywhere.[3] [*AO1 for advancing the argument with a judiciously selected quote; AO2 for the close analysis of the language and for discussing how structure shapes meaning*].
- The Greek philosopher Aristotle argued that a truly dramatic work of fiction must abide by the unities – that is, it must take place in one location, in a tight space of time, and involve one key event. Thus the

tight setting of the play in this one room allows Priestley to heighten the drama.

- Moreover, the sole on-stage location also complements the detective genre. The sense of entrapment and claustrophobia conjured by the location reflects the characters' entrapment in their historic actions. The way the lighting turns from 'pink and intimate' to 'brighter and harder' post Goole's arrival symbolises the transparency Goole brings about with his detective work. Finally, if detective fictions are stories about stories, the singularity of the location is apt: the action has already taken place historically; Goole is simply reconstructing what has happened into a single narrative. [*AO1 for advancing the argument with a judiciously selected quote; AO2 for the close analysis of the language*].

Theme/Paragraph Two: Priestley also uses the locations in the play as a means to explore social class and tensions. The dining room is a space of luxury, though Goole intrudes on this space and forces its occupants to consider the social injustices that have facilitated this luxury. Other spaces invoked in the audience's mind – Birling's factory, the Palace Bar – are also used to explore social class.

- Priestley takes pains to draw attention to the luxuriousness of the dining-room: it is described as 'heavily comfortable;' and the table is decked out with items that are shorthand for extravagant living – 'champagne glasses.... [a] decanter of port, [a] cigar box.' Indeed, the parlour-maid Edna, whose opening two words are subservience distilled ('yes, ma'am'), and who seems almost as inconsequential to the Birlings as just another item of furniture, is all but relegated to another facet of the settings: the domestic who, like the champagne and cigars, functions merely to highlight the wealth of her employers.[4] [*AO1 for advancing the argument with a judiciously selected quote; AO2 for the close analysis of the language*].

- As mentioned, the setting is at first presented in a 'pink and intimate light.' This tint highlights not only the comfort, but also how this elite space is removed both physically and psychologically from the struggles of the working class – those in this bubble (Edna excluded) see the world though a rose-tinted ('pink'), self-deluding lens. That the light gets harsher on Goole's arrival does not just capture a sense of secrets coming to light; it represents also how their bubble has been pierced by a messenger with tales of suffering from a different social class – the 'millions and millions of Eva Smiths and John Smiths.' [*AO1 for advancing the argument with a judiciously selected quote; AO2 for the close analysis of the language and for discussing how structure shapes meaning*].

- Yet while the dining-room may be the only location that appears on-stage, there are other locations that are invoked, and practically all are sites of tension between the working and ruling classes. Birling's 'factory' is an archetypal Marxian battleground between workers and employers, and the workers' demand to have 'rates raised' an archetypal skirmish.[5] Conversely, the Palace Bar, a locale where a cross section of society seem to rendezvous, is a place of

sexual, not economic, exploitation. Eric encounters
Renton there in an incident that ends in a possible
rape. Yet the exploitation is more pervasive: as Gerald
observes, when he first encountered Renton, she was
being sexually harassed at the bar by an Alderman
who 'had wedged her into a corner with [his] obscene
fat carcass.' [*AO1 for advancing the argument with a
judiciously selected quote*].

**Theme/Paragraph Three: Setting is also used to
explore the tensions between private realities and
the public reputations: the setting, after all, is a
private, domestic scene, yet it has been recreated
in a public venue: a theatre.**

- Near the end of Act 3, in the wake of the revelations
  concerning Eric, Birling voices exasperation that his
  children are failing to 'see the difference between...
  stuff like this coming out in a private and a downright
  public scandal.' Within the fictional universe, this
  distinction of course makes sense: Birling is anxious
  that this incriminating information, currently known
  by just an intimate few, might become public, and
  thus tarnish the family's reputation. However, for the
  audience, there is no small irony, for in a sense, there
  is no difference: these private revelations *are* public
  revelations; the information has come out in both the
  privacy of the Birlings' home, but also the public
  realm of the theatre hall. [*AO1 for advancing the
  argument with a judiciously selected quote; AO3 for
  placing the play in its artistic context*].
- Priestley may be giving a sly, sardonic wink to the

audience when he has Birling panickedly claim he has to 'cover this up as soon as [he] can.' After all, as soon as the theatre curtain went up, there had ceased to be any 'cover' in the first place. [*AO1 for advancing the argument with a judiciously selected quote; AO2 for the close analysis of the language*].

• Therefore Priestley is using the tension between the deeply private on-stage setting, and the fact his fiction is a piece of theatre, and thus intrinsically public, to invite us to consider the degree to which in general private crimes remain hidden to the public; the degree to which people's reputations diverge from their private, sordid realities.

Conclusion

"Although *An Inspector Calls* was written in the mid 1940s, it is of course set in 1912. This choice of historical setting is a tool Priestley uses to cudgel Birling with dramatic irony: Birling describes the *Titanic*, a symbol of capitalist excess, as 'absolutely unsinkable,' yet the audience knows it had sunk later that same year; Birling claims 'the Germans don't want war,' yet the audience knows that the cataclysmic great war broke out in 1914. This draws attention to another form of setting Priestley uses – *historical* setting – and how he uses this to subvert Birling's worldview. Priestley's choices regarding setting thus prove to be multifaceted: a tool that by turns advances ideological arguments and heightens tension and drama."

8) A photo of Priestley's home in Highgate, London. Copyright © Spudgun67

ESSAY PLAN SIX

HOW FAR DOES PRIESTLEY PRESENT SHEILA AS A GOOD JUDGE OF CHARACTER?

Introduction

"In July 1945, the month *An Inspector Calls* premiered, the UK was holding a general election – a character judgement writ large in which the populace was asked to cast a decision not only on its politicians (Churchill or Atlee; fiscal conservatism or robust spending), but also on its own personality.[1] Against this backdrop, Priestley's play dramatises a domestic scene in which this dynamic plays out on a micro level: characters are invited to assess and reassess one another, yet also themselves. Sheila's clear-eyed judgement of Goole speaks to a perceptiveness, and she also proves capable of seeing through Gerald's dissembling. However, she misjudges her parents, underestimating the extent of their intransigence."

Theme/Paragraph One: She seems to be a good judge of Goole – most specifically, his ability to draw people out and dominate interactions. There seems to be a symbiosis here, since Goole is particularly apt in reading Sheila, too.[2]

- Whereas Goole is largely treated with scepticism and disdain when he first arrives at the Birling household, Sheila quickly comes to comprehend Goole's true nature: that he is not someone who can be easily denied. This is emphatically communicated at the close of Act 1 when, after Goole momentarily leaves the room, Gerald states his intentions to dissemble about his affair, and Sheila asserts that 'he *knows*. Of course he knows' – the italics on the first 'knows' and its repetition underscoring the futility of resisting Goole. Indeed, that Sheila is correct in her assessment is given structural emphasis: she makes the assertion at the close of Act 1, and the second act starts with Goole addressing Gerald with a knowing and weightily monosyllabic 'well?' – he is already privy to the truth. [*AO1 for advancing the argument with a judiciously selected quote; AO2 for the close analysis of the language and for discussing how form and structure shapes meaning*].

- Sheila's understanding of the futility of resisting Goole is perhaps best exemplified in her imploration to Mrs Birling that she must refrain from 'build[ing] up a kind of wall between us and that girl,' for 'the inspector will just break it down.' Sure enough, this proves a sound judgement of Goole's character, since, as he then proceeds to squeeze each of the cast in turn, he amply demonstrates his ability to overcome resistance. [*AO1 for advancing the argument with a judiciously selected quote*].

- Indeed, there appears to be a symbiosis between Sheila and Goole: in the same way she can divine his character, he seems particularly capable of divining hers. This is demonstrated when Goole finds himself explaining Sheila's mindset to Gerald Act 2: 'She feels responsible. And if she leaves us now... she'll be alone with her responsibility.' [*AO1 for advancing the argument with a judiciously selected quote*].

Theme/Paragraph Two: Sheila proves particularly good at discerning when others are dissembling. She crucially intuits that Gerald has been deceiving her.

- That Sheila is a particularly sharp judge of character is perhaps best shown through her deep understanding of her fiancée, Gerald. Even though she had perhaps been denying it to herself, she had always on some level known he was capable of an affair; after all, her 'half serious, half playful' reference to 'last summer, when [Gerald] never came near [her]' at the start of the play hints that she harbours these suspicions even prior to Goole's arrival. However, the true indicator that she understood what Gerald was capable of comes when, in response to Gerald's blink-and-you'll-miss-it lack of composure after hearing Daisy Renton's name, she feels confident enough to point the finger: 'You not only knew her, but you knew her very well.' Of course, Sheila proves to be correct – Gerald did indeed have an affair with

Renton – thereby proving Sheila's perceptiveness. [*AO1 for advancing the argument with a judiciously selected quote; AO2 for the close analysis of the language*].

- The trope of a dark truth lurking behind a polished facade was a particularly prevalent one in the 1940s, perhaps borne of a scepticism in human nature in the wake of war's horrors. Jorge Luis Borges's 'Theme of the Traitor and Hero' (1944), for instance, explores the life of one Fergus Kilpatrick, who had been remembered as a hero, but who had in fact been a traitor to his people. That Sheila is cast as an individual capable of seeing through such veneers is testament to her powers of judgement. [*AO3 for placing the text in literary-historical context*].

Theme/Paragraph Three: While sound in her assessments of Goole and Gerald, Sheila proves a poor judge of her parents' characters: she seems to believe that she might be able to alter their mindsets, thus radically underestimating their ideological intransigence.

- In the play's third act, in the wake of Goole's departure, Sheila appears to take on the mantle of Goole's ideology: she has, by this point, internalised his views with regards to social justice and heightened responsibility and wishes to impress them on her parents. To achieve this end, Sheila tries a number of techniques: sarcasm in the face of her parents attempts to minimize their actions ('I suppose we're all nice people'); incredulity ('you're just beginning to pretend all over'); and outright castigation ('don't let's start dodging and pretending').[3] [*AO1 for advancing the argument with a judiciously selected quote; AO2 for the close analysis of the language*].

- However, the sheer fact that Sheila even attempts to proselytize to her parents points to a fundamental misjudgement on Sheila's part, for her parents are beyond reform.[4] This is evidenced when, in response to Sheila's (and Eric's) warnings, Birling merely attempts to dismiss them: 'go to bed then, and don't stand there being hysterical.' By physically demanding his children no long 'stand there,' he is not only literally attempting to get rid of them, but he is also metaphorically telling them to stand down their argument. Therefore, the fact that Sheila should even attempt to penetrate the minds of 'hard headed' Birling and his wife points to an error of judgement on her part. [*AO1 for advancing the argument with a judiciously selected quote; AO2 for the close analysis of the language*].

Theme/Paragraph Four: It appears as though Sheila has historically shied away from much introspection, and thus has not really taken time to assess her own character. However, over the course of the play, she seems better able to judge her own character flaws than any other of the dinner-party's attendees.

- It is striking that after Sheila recounts how she had had Eva Smith fired from Milwards in Act 1, while now exhibiting distress, she also makes clear that, at the time, she had avoided allowing her cruelty to lead to introspection: she simply says that Smith had 'looked as if she could take care of herself' and that she thus 'couldn't be sorry for her.' This comment implies not that Sheila was deluding herself with regards to her own character, but instead that she was simply avoiding any kind of introspection at all in the first place. [*AO1 for advancing the argument with a judiciously selected quote*].

- However, once this event is dredged back up by Goole, Sheila *does* prove capable of passing sound judgements on her own character and personal history, and is able to perceive the cruelty of her actions with clarity: 'I know I'm to blame – and I'm desperately sorry.' This clarity persists throughout the play: when Eric in Act 3 asserts that they all 'did what they did' – a deceptively simple tautology, which emphasises that their actions should not to be minimised, but pondered on deeply – Sheila agrees wholeheartedly: 'Eric's absolutely right.' [*AO1 for advancing the argument with a judiciously selected quote; AO2 for the close analysis of the language; AO3 for placing the text in historical context*].

- Indeed, that the Birling parents seem so incapable of judging their own actions with any kind of distance – Mrs Birling's self-deluding assertion that she 'had done no more than my duty' is a case in point – further emphasises how Sheila is, comparatively speaking, a sound judge of her own character and actions. [*AO1 for advancing the argument with a judiciously selected quote*].

Conclusion

"Although the final twist, which sees Birling receive a call informing him that the police are *en route* to question them about a suicide, is far from clear cut, it at least hints at the possibility that Goole was a kind of supernatural soothsayer.[5] With this twist in mind, one might look back to Sheila's earlier comment that 'there was something curious about [Goole]' as yet another signpost pointing to her powers of judgement: she seems to intuit his potentially supernatural quality. Certainly it appears that her ability to judge character only really falters when it comes to her parents, who prove far more set in their ideological ways than Sheila had supposed."

9) Sheila (left) and Mrs Birling in tense conversation. The A. D. Players. Copyright © Orlando Arriaga

ESSAY PLAN SEVEN

HOW DOES PRIESTLEY EXPLORE THE SIGNIFICANCE OF SOCIAL CLASS IN AN INSPECTOR CALLS?

INTRODUCTION

"In the wake of the 1917 Russian Revolution – a revolution inspired by the writings of Karl Marx – there was a heightened contentiousness on the topic of social class, and, in particular, the idea that class divisions might lead to abuses of power.[1] Priestley, an ardent left-wing thinker, deploys *An Inspector Calls* as a means of exploring social class in British society. Whereas Birling, a member of a powerful employer class, exposes how those at the top of the food chain use their social status to broker power, Goole functions as a messenger, shedding light on the raw deal faced by those in the working classes. Yet Priestley's use of setting, too, becomes a means of exploring social class, be it the Birlings' home, which exhibits the spoils reserved for "the haves", or the Palace Bar, the site of sexual exploitation for the "have nots.""

Theme/Paragraph One: Priestley uses Birling to explore how, for those at the top of the social food chain, social class is significant insofar as it is perceived as a means of brokering power and insulating themselves from accountability.

- It is striking that following the arrival of Goole – an individual who, due to his purported association with the law, is understood by the Birlings' to possess a degree of power – Birling is quick to convey his social status: 'I was an alderman for years – and Lord Mayor two years ago – and I'm still on the bench.' The litany of dashes, which indicate a kind of pausing for effect, are intended to imbue these details with gravitas: they are rhetorical invitations to take his social clout seriously. Implicit in this grandstanding is the mentality that Birling's social standing should be enough to cow Goole and neutralise any power he might have over Birling. [*AO1 for advancing the argument with a judiciously selected quote; AO2 for the close analysis of the language and for discussing how form shapes meaning*].

- As Goole's questions become increasingly forceful, so too do Birling's efforts to deploy his social class to neutralise Goole: he observes that the 'chief constable' is 'a close friend,' a detail that is intended to not-so-subtly suggest that, by manipulating his social connections, Birling might be capable of endangering Goole's employment. That social class might be used as a means to insulate those at the top from accountability is a mentality also seemingly shared by

Mrs Birling, who independently brings up her husband's social standing while attempting to rein Goole in: 'My husband was Lord Mayor only two years ago.' [*AO1 for advancing the argument with a judiciously selected quote*].

- By dramatising this mentality, Priestley explores how social class is significant in its implications for the rule of law: it is as a malignant force wielded by the ruling class to undermine the rightful course of justice. It is important, however, that Goole is *not* cowed by the Birlings' social status. When he admonishes Birling that 'public men... have responsibilities as well as privileges,' one might hear Priestley's own distaste for how the ruling class abuse their position without consequence. [*AO1 for advancing the argument with a judiciously selected quote; AO2 for the close analysis of the language*].

Theme/Paragraph Two: Priestley uses Goole to explore how social class is significant for society's least-well-off: he gives voice to the hardships faced by the working classes, forcing the Birlings et al. to acknowledge the toxicity of class divisions.[2]

- At one point, Mrs Birling, discussing the young girl that Goole told them had wound up in the infirmary, asserts that she does not think they 'can understand why the girl committed suicide,' adding suggestively: 'Girls of that class.' Not only does the phrase 'that class' hint at Mrs Birling's disdain – merely giving this social class a name beyond 'that' seems unsavoury – but the comment as a whole reveals an utter lack of empathy for how the working classes live. [*AO1 for advancing the argument with a judiciously selected quote; AO2 for the close analysis of the language*].

- Although it remains unclear whether Eva Smith/Daisy Renton was in fact just one person, Goole's exploration of this woman's life is used to enumerate the hardships that stem from working class existence. Indeed, Goole discusses Smith's/Renton's plight in strikingly personal terms: for instance, when discussing her existence post Birling & Co., he talks about her having 'no home to go back to' and finding herself with 'few friends, lonely, half-starved...[and] feeling desperate.' That this suffering ought to be considered the consequence of belonging to the working class is made clear when Goole then strongly implies that these conditions are created intentionally so employers can source 'cheap labour.' [*AO1 for advancing the argument with a judiciously selected quote; AO2 for the close analysis of the language*].

- While Goole is talking about one individual, her plight is intended to be construed as an insight into her social class as a whole: the 'millions and millions of Eva Smiths and John Smiths.' Therefore, by shining light on Smith's/Renton's life, Priestley has Goole draw attention to what he perceived to be social class's significance in fuelling division and suffering in society. [*AO1 for advancing the argument with a judiciously selected quote*].

Theme/Paragraph Three: Priestley uses setting as a means to explore how social class brings about discrepancies in wealth, but also how it causes tension and exploitation in public places.

- The Birling's home itself – specifically its dining-room, since this is the only space ever evoked on stage – is deployed by Priestley to explore how social class brings about discrepancies in wealth. The lavishness of the room, with all its trappings of wealth (Priestley cites, for instance, the 'champagne glasses...[and] decanter of port, cigar box and cigarettes'), showcases the luxuries reserved for ruling classes – luxuries that are established at the very outset for structural effect. [*AO1 for advancing the argument with a judiciously selected quote; AO2 for discussing how structure shapes meaning*].

- The maid, Edna, is a particularly telling addition to the play's *dramatis personae*: the degree to which she blends into the background, and the subservience distilled into what little she says ('yes, ma'am' is her opening line), seems to suggest that she has, in the Birlings' eyes, been relegated to just another item of the furniture – she is just another signifier of their wealth and status. Indeed, Sheila's admonishment that 'these girls aren't cheap labour – they're people' – a comment that refers to factory workers – has no small irony with regards to Edna: as a result of her social class, she is certainly not treated as a person by any of the Birlings, Sheila included. [*AO1 for advancing the argument with a judiciously selected quote; AO2 for the close analysis of the language*].

- The centrality of setting in *An Inspector Calls* as a means to explore the significance of social class extends beyond the dining-room, however. If Edna's position in the household hints at tension between social classes, these tensions are explored in far greater depth in those off-stage spaces discussed in the play. Birling's factory, for instance, is the archetypal site of Marxian class struggle, and this plays out with the acrimonious wage dispute that precipitates Eva Smith's dismissal. Social class is responsible for a different type of abuse at the Palace Bar – a space where the ruling class appears to sexually exploit the working classes. Eric's behaviour is not an isolated incident: one need look no further than the abusive conduct of the Alderman who 'had wedged [Renton] into a corner with [his] obscene fat carcass.' [*AO1 for advancing the argument with a judiciously selected quote; AO3 for placing the text in historical context*].

Conclusion

"At one point in Charlie Chaplin's iconic 1936 film, *Modern Times*, Chaplin's tramp is swallowed whole by a machine then progresses through its gear-filled guts. If this is a metaphor for how social class can lead to exploitation, Priestley's play has a similar message, but with none of the slapstick humour to temper its 'fire and blood and anguish.' Through the behaviour of the older Birlings, Goole's dispatches from the world of the working classes, and settings that exemplify class tensions, Priestley explores his worldview in which social class is the root cause of abuses of power, exploitation, and dehumanisation."

10) A mural in Vevey, Switzerland. It is a recreation of the iconic scene in Chaplin's *Modern Times* in which Chaplin's tramp is swallowed into a factory's machine.

ESSAY PLAN EIGHT

HOW FAR DOES PRIESTLEY PRESENT MRS BIRLING AS MOTIVATED BY PRIDE?

INTRODUCTION

"The early twentieth century's women's suffrage movement – a movement predicated on women taking pride in their womanhood and demanding the vote – brought about rare cohesion between social classes: by 1912, the year in which *An Inspector Calls* is set, Millicent Fawcett's National Union of Women's Suffrage Societies had amassed over 21,000 members from all walks of life. Given that Mrs Birling is a member of a charitable committee designed to aid women in distress, one might assume she would be animated by a similar sororal pride.[1] Yet it appears Mrs Birling is in fact animated by pride of a different kind: pride in her self-conception as an upstanding individual; in her family's reputation; and in belonging to the upper classes."[2]

Theme/Paragraph One: It appears as though Mrs Birling takes pride in her self-conception as a morally upstanding individual. As a result, in the face of Goole's accusations that she has behaved immorally, she takes pains to contend in response that her actions were morally sound.

- When, in Act 2, Goole starts to delve into Mrs Birling's behaviour on her charitable committee, Goole explicitly seeks to cast Mrs Birling's decision to withhold money from the individual he asserts to be Smith/Renton as immoral: he says that he thinks she 'did something terribly wrong.' Yet Mrs Birling is unwilling to concede that she had transgressed: she contends that 'in spite of what's happened to the girl since, I consider I did my duty.' One might argue that she is motivated here by a desire to maintain her self-conception as a charitable, upstanding individual: a conception that, given she is a 'prominent member' on a charitable committee, one might imagine she takes pride in. [AO1 *for advancing the argument with a judiciously selected quote*].

- Strikingly, even after Goole informs her that the pregnant woman's child was in fact Eric's, Mrs Birling still refuses to budge in her assessment of her own actions. In response to Sheila's comment that Goole had induced them to confess, Mrs Birling forcefully argues that 'he certainly didn't make me confess.' Given that the word 'confess' implies the divulgence of a transgression, Mrs Birling's disavowal of the term demonstrates her utter unwillingness to construe her behaviour as immoral: her pride in her self-conception as an upstanding individual will not let her do so. [*AO1 for advancing the argument with a judiciously selected quote; AO2 for the close analysis of the language*].

Theme/Paragraph Two: Mrs Birling appears also to be motivated by a sense of loyalty to Eric and a broader sense of family preservation. However, this might ultimately boil down to her anxieties regarding how these sordid revelations might harm her family in the public arena, and thus her pride in her family's standing and reputation.

- Prior to informing Mrs Birling that Eric was the father of the pregnant woman's baby, Goole artfully lures Mrs Birling into laying the blame on the father's shoulders: she proclaims that the 'young man' in question must undergo the ritual humiliation of being 'compelled to confess in public his responsibility.' However, once she realises that Eric is in fact the young man in question, she reneges on this mentality, and this line of thinking vanishes from her lips. [*AO1 for advancing the argument with a judiciously selected quote*].

- While Mrs Birling is clearly motivated, then, by a desire to shield Eric from accountability, this seems ultimately to boil down to pride in her family name. A notable moment that points in this direction is when, after Eric lays into Mrs Birling for withholding funds from Renton, Mrs Birling becomes 'very distressed,' and even finds herself stutteringly pleading with Eric: 'No – Eric – please – I didn't know – I didn't

understand.' It seems inescapable that this is *not*
moral distress, since, as mentioned, she later refuses to
label her account of her conduct a confession, and
reiterates near the end of the play that she believes she
'had done no more than [her] duty.' Rather, given Mrs
Birling's seeming complicity with Birling's desire to
implement a cover up ('be quiet so that your father
can decide what we ought to do'), her distress seems to
be motivated by the notion that Eric's dirty laundry
might be aired in public, and that this might be critical
for her family's reputation and pride. [*AO1 for
advancing the argument with a judiciously selected
quote; AO2 for the close analysis of the language*].

**Theme/Paragraph Three: Mrs Birling seems to be
motivated by a kind of ideology of decorum: a
conviction that all behaviour should be conducted
in a certain way befitting one's class.[3] In a sense,
this indicates that she takes pride in being part of
the ruling classes.**

- Early on in the play, it is clear that there is yet another
  force motivating Mrs Birling's behaviour: a loyalty to a
  code of decorum that stipulates how individuals
  belonging to her rarefied social class ought to behave.
  This is exhibited time and again in the play's opening
  sequence – a structural choice that grants the trait
  particular emphasis. For instance, she chastises Birling
  for his lack of dignity in complimenting the chef (she
  asserts 'reproachfully' how 'you're not suppose to say
  such things'); and she dresses down Sheila for her use
  of off-colour language ('What an expression, Sheila').

Her scandalized reaction to learning of Eric's drinking habit – she is described as 'staggered' – is a continuation of this theme. [*AO1 for advancing the argument with a judiciously selected quote; AO2 for the close analysis of the language and for discussing how structure shapes meaning*].

- Her greatest opprobrium, however, is reserved for Goole, who, by refusing to act with suitable deference to his social betters, is subverting the rules of decorum that Mrs Birling believes ought to regulate his behaviour. When, after Goole's departure, she bemoans his conduct – 'his manner was quite extraordinary; so – so rude – and assertive' – one can hear the sense of scandal dripping from her staccato words. [*AO1 for advancing the argument with a judiciously selected quote; AO2 for the close analysis of the language*].

- That Mrs Birling abides so religiously to these class-based codes of conduct, and stipulates that her family, and indeed everyone else, do so too, indicates a pride in her upper class roots. Indeed, that she in fact married down (the stage directions describe her as her husband's 'social superior') may perhaps have caused her to redouble her investment in these codes of conduct that continue to mark her out as belonging to what she perceives as the most rarefied stock. [*AO1 for advancing the argument with a judiciously selected quote*].

Theme/Paragraph Four: However, while some of Mrs Birling's behaviour might stem from a prideful desire to have those from lower social strata respect her upper-class standing, one may

identify some outright vindictiveness towards working class people underpinning her behaviour.

- Shortly after Goole's arrival, Mrs Birling betrays an outright disdain for the working class: she claims that she could not possibly 'understand why the girl committed suicide' before leadingly adding just a fragment of a sentence that ends with a dash: 'Girls of that class –.' The implication is clear: Mrs Birling believes women in the working classes lack the sophistication, perhaps even the sheer humanity, that is the necessary prerequisite for her to empathise with them. [*AO1 for advancing the argument with a judiciously selected quote; AO2 for discussing how form shapes meaning*].

- This motif appears again when discussing her decision to withhold aid from the woman Goole purports to be Eva Smith/Daisy Renton: she asserts that Smith/Renton 'was claiming elaborate fine feelings and scruples that were simply absurd in a girl in her position.' Again, while this might be in part borne from a pride in her upper class pedigree, and a desire to have the lower classes pay homage, it seems inescapable that the comment was motivated at least in part by outright vindictiveness: a dehumanising conviction that women in that social class should not only not be claiming 'fine feelings,' but also that they simply cannot truly feel these 'fine feelings' at all.[4] [*AO1 for advancing the argument with a judiciously selected quote; AO2 for the close analysis of the language*].

- It ought to be noted that this dehumanising attitude towards the working class pervaded the society

Priestley was portraying. For example, whereas middle and upper class suffragettes were treated with restraint by police in the 1910s, the working class among them were treated far harsher, as Lady Lytton discovered in 1910 when she attended a protest disguised as a working class woman, and wound up in prison for a fortnight undergoing punishing force feedings. [*AO1 for advancing the argument with a judiciously selected quote; AO2 for the close analysis of the language; AO3 for placing the text in historical context*].

Conclusion

"In some respects, the very premise of this question is a red-herring, for in many ways Mrs Birling is *not* a motivated individual, but a distinctly passive one. During the entirety of Goole's presence during Act 1, Mrs Birling is absent – a structural choice that highlights her relative lack of consequence. Moreover, more so than any other character, her transgression against Smith/Renton is uniquely passive: she is withholding money. Finally, in the run-up to the play's denouement, it is Gerald and Birling attempting to salvage things, not Mrs Birling. Nevertheless, when she *is* rallied to render a verdict or takes a course of action, it is true that it is often motivated by pride in one guise or another."[5]

11) A photo capturing the play's dramatic finale, with Mr Birling receiving the phone call, and Mrs Birling watching on. A. D. Players. Copyright © Orlando Arriaga

ESSAY PLAN NINE

HOW DOES PRIESTLEY USE THE CHARACTER OF THE INSPECTOR TO SUGGEST WAYS THAT SOCIETY MIGHT BE IMPROVED?

INTRODUCTION

"Given that *An Inspector Calls* was written in the immediate wake of the atrocities of the second world war, it is perhaps unsurprising that Priestley uses the play as an ideological vehicle to put forward an alternative vision of how society might be organised. Goole, Priestley's chief voice of change, offers a left-leaning, socialistic paradigm as a means to redress society's abuses.[1] More than that, however, by going out of the way to hold the Birlings et al. responsible not just for their legal crimes, but their *social* crimes, he also posits an alternative method of administering justice."

Theme/Paragraph One: Goole's prosecution of the purported suicide suggests a system of justice

that assigns blame to those who abuse their power (not just those who committed technical legal wrongdoing), and tacitly implies that this ought to be how justice should be executed in a fairer society.

- As Goole grills Birling on the circumstances surrounding Eva Smith's dismissal in Act 1, Birling bluntly puts forward a rationale for firing Smith – 'it's my duty to keep labour costs down' – and insists that he 'can't accept any responsibility' for what happened to Smith since. In a sense, Birling is right: within a capitalist economy, reducing costs is king; and, legally speaking, Birling is *not* responsible for Smith's suicide. However, by aggressively taking Birling to task all the same, and forcefully pointing to Birling's *moral* responsibility for sending Smith down a dark path – 'You made her pay a heavy price' – Goole is tacitly positing an alternative system of justice: one in which people are held responsible not just for their legal crimes, but their moral crimes, too. [AO1 *for advancing the argument with a judiciously selected quote; AO2 for the close analysis of the language*].
- Goole pursues other members of the Birling family in much the same way. Sheila did not commit a *legal* crime when she sought to have a young woman sacked from Milwards, and neither did Mrs Birling when she withheld funds from a pregnant woman who had solicited her committee for aid; nevertheless, Goole takes pains to lay moral blame at their doorsteps, and thus, in so doing, holds them both responsible: 'Each

of you helped to kill her.' [*AO1 for advancing the
argument with a judiciously selected quote*].

- If Goole is tacitly suggesting a more expansive means
of administering justice that seeks to prosecute moral
transgressions, he is also pitching a form of justice that
can more robustly hold those in power accountable.
Birling attempts to use his social capital to muzzle
Goole: for instance, he tacitly threatens Goole's job by
menacingly noting that he is 'close friends' with the
police chief. Yet, by utterly disregarding these
comments, Goole invites the audience to envisage a
society in which those in power are unable to insulate
themselves from reproach. [*AO1 for advancing the
argument with a judiciously selected quote*].

**Theme/Paragraph Two: However, Goole does not
simply suggest a system that better holds abusers
to account; he also actively offers a more socialist
vision of society that would ward off these abuses
in the first place.**

- Early in the play, Birling – the arch capitalist – takes
time to deride the socialist vision of society in which
'everybody has to look after everybody else,'
dismissing its proponents as 'cranks.' Priestley
however, by choosing to have Goole arrive shortly
after this comment, uses the play's structure to make a
point: while the likes of Birling may feel his
worldview is in ascendancy, its socialist opponents are
rallying. [*AO1 for advancing the argument with a
judiciously selected quote; AO2 for discussing how
structure shapes meaning*].

- At first, Goole does not put forward a fully-fledged socialist treatise. Instead, he *hints* at favouring a more socialist society. For instance, when discussing Eva Smith's mission to secure a higher wage, his pointed comment that 'it's better to ask for the earth than to take it' seems not only to establish empathy with Eva Smith's efforts, but also to obliquely decry the capitalists' greed that had led to those at the top of the food chain commandeering the world's resources ('the earth') as opposed to divvying them up fairly and equitably. [*AO1 for advancing the argument with a judiciously selected quote; AO2 for the close analysis of the language*].

- However, when Goole later takes his leave, he does finally put forward a socialist worldview in starker terms: 'We don't live alone. We are members of one body. We are responsible for each other.' The rhetorical repetition of 'we' that punctuates this staccato string of short sentences emphasises the central point: that, in Goole's view, humanity would be better off if we dispensed of the primacy of the individual in favour of a collective 'we' mentality. [*AO1 for advancing the argument with a judiciously selected quote; AO2 for the close analysis of the language and for discussing how form shapes meaning*].

- Priestley himself believed ardently that a move towards a more socialistic society in which all would be 'responsible for each other' would represent a positive change. Indeed, Priestley's writings have been cited as a factor that aided the Labour party's landslide electoral victory in July 1945 (the same month *An Inspector Calls* premiered) – a political shift that led to the modern welfare state. [*AO3 for placing the text in historical context*].

Theme/Paragraph Three: Given that Priestley is an advocate of Goole's worldview, the fact that the Birling children prove far more amenable to Goole's influence tacitly suggests that society would be better off giving the younger generation, who are less intellectually stuck in their ways, more sway.

- At one point in Act 2, in response to Mrs Birling's observation that Goole seems to have made a great impression on Sheila, Goole remarks simply that the young are 'more impressionable.' This is certainly borne out through the course of the play: whereas the older Birlings remain impervious to Goole's views – Mrs Birling, for instance, maintains till the end that she had merely done her 'duty' – both Eric and Sheila appear to have far more internalised Goole's sense of morality. This is particularly true for Sheila who, by the play's final act, has fully taken on the messaging Goole has imparted, and who, even in light of the revelations that Goole was not a police officer and there had been no suicide, is still unwilling to minimise the selfishness of their collective actions: 'If it didn't end tragically, then that's lucky for us. But it might have done.' [*AO1 for advancing the argument with a judiciously selected quote; AO2 for the close analysis of the language*].

- In a sense, by demonstrating Goole's success in enlightening the young with his socialist-informed morality, it might be argued that Priestley, via Goole, is suggesting that society would be better off if the younger, less intractable members of society were granted greater power.

Theme/Paragraph Four: Goole is in a sense a story-teller. When we examine *how* Priestley uses Goole to suggest changes to society, one can see that Goole's flair for putting forward these changes – whether he is doing so tacitly or explicitly – ultimately stems from this capacity for story-telling.

- In the play's final throes, after the dinner attendees learn a woman had not been brought into the infirmary earlier that day, Gerald realises it is entirely possible that, contrary to what Goole had told them, their transgressions might *not* have been levelled against just one woman; rather, it might have been 'four or five different girls.' Indeed, even though the play's final twist might tempt us to reach for a supernatural explanation – namely, that the suicide Birling has just heard about was Eva Smith/Daisy Renton, and Goole had predicted the future – this is left unresolved. It may have been someone else entirely, or the call itself might have been a hoax. [*AO1 for advancing the argument with a judiciously selected quote*].
- One might argue that the dinner-party's attendees prior belief in Eva Smith/Daisy Renton's existence as one person ultimately boiled down to Goole's power as a story teller; his ability to vividly bring

Smith/Renton to life. When he fleshes out Smith/Renton's back-story earlier in the play – discussing, for instance, how her 'parents were dead,' or how, after leaving Birling & Co., she was left 'lonely, half-starved...[and] feeling desperate' – his ability to evoke her emotional state ensures that, whether or not she actually exists, she feels immutably real to the Birlings. [*AO1 for advancing the argument with a judiciously selected quote; AO2 for the close analysis of the language*].

- It has already been noted that Goole is proactively suggesting societal changes that, for example, would bring about a more sustainable existence for the working class. Yet the way Priestley ensures Goole's messaging packs a punch ultimately comes down to Goole's skills as a raconteur; his ability to convey the stakes.

Conclusion

"Priestley's polemical message, communicated via Goole, seems to be that positive societal change will come about through less capitalism, and more socialism; and through a more robust system of justice that holds more wide-ranging abuses to account.[2] The play's ending, by invoking suicide, is undoubtedly bleak; however, the irresolution built into the denouement may be Priestley's hint that the window of opportunity has not closed altogether; that there is still time to heed Goole's message and to reform society accordingly."

12) The inscription on a pillar within a church in
Hubberholme, UK. Copyright © Freddie Phillips

ENDNOTES

ESSAY PLAN ONE

1. Capitalism and communism are hugely significant terms, but can be tricky to define. I'll try and do so briefly.

   Capitalism is a philosophy that suggests that a society should be run on the basis of the free market. Goods and services are provided by private companies, and the prices of goods and services depend solely on supply and demand. In capitalist societies, governments tend to intervene far less, and keep spending to a minimum.

   In contrast, communism suggests that all wealth and property should be shared equally among the population, and all the means of production should be owned by the community.

   Socialism, another term you will encounter, is a less extreme cousin of communism. It advocates for government to tax the rich more heavily, and to spend more readily on the poor, in order to redistribute wealth, with the aim of creating a more equitable society.

   These definitions should be treated only as a jumping off point, since these terms are far more complex than these short definitions give them credit. There is also frequently a wide gulf between these ideas as theories, and how they pan out when implemented in real life.

2. If you are abrogating responsibilities, it basically means you're evading or dodging responsibilities.

   A dogma is a formal set of beliefs. So you might have communist dogma, capitalist dogma, socialist dogma, catholic dogma – and so on!

3. *Laissez-faire* is a French term and it means 'to leave alone.' It is often used by economists to describe how the capitalist system works: the government is encouraged to simply leave things alone, and let the free market determine how things pan out.

4. You may well know this already, but war between Britain and Germany broke out in July 1914 – this was of course World War One. You may well also know that the Titanic sank in April 1912.

5. Someone's bona fides are their credentials.

   To transgress is to go beyond or exceed what is permissible.

6. The word sardonic is very similar to sarcastic – a sardonic comment is usually a sarcastic one.

7. By an equivocal position, I mean an ambiguous/unclear position; a position that is somewhere between the two extremes.

8. If something is analogous to something else, it means that it is similar to that thing.
9. *En route* is a French phrase. To be *en route* somewhere means to be on the way somewhere.

ESSAY PLAN TWO

1. A seminal work is a work that is particularly important or influential.
2. To appropriate money is to steal it.
3. To dissemble is to put on an act.
4. A tautology is basically when the same thing is said twice.
5. If something is latent, it means it exists yet is hidden or dormant.
   To keep mum is to keep silent.
   If something is moot, it means it's irrelevant.
6. If you are levelling opprobrium at something it means you are harshly critical of something.
7. To capitulate is to surrender.
8. *Dramatis personae* is a Latin expression and it refers to the characters in a play.

ESSAY PLAN THREE

1. If someone is a charlatan, it means they are a fraud.
2. If something is egregious, it means it is remarkably or astoundingly bad.
3. An interlocutor is the person being spoken to. So if I'm on the phone, the person on the other end of the line would be my interlocutor.

ESSAY PLAN FOUR

1. To be nonchalant means to be calm and relaxed.
   A triviality is something small and inconsequential.
2. To parse someone's views is to break their views down into comprehensible units.

ESSAY PLAN FIVE

1. Aristotle was a Greek philosopher whose work has been hugely influential on Western society. In *The Poetics*, he argues that dramatic pieces ought to abide by the three unities. The first is the unity of space: the drama should all take place in one location. The second is the unity of time: the drama

must all take place in a tight period of time. The third is the unity of action: the drama must involve one solitary action.

    An Inspector Calls definitely abides by the unity of time and the unity of space. Whether or not it abides by the unity of action is not so clear-cut. Goole's act of interrogation could be considered one unified action. However, one could alternatively argue that the play covers the multiple historical actions undertaken by each of the Birlings and Gerald.

2. You may know already that a synonym is a word that has a similar or identical meaning to another word; for example, joyous is a synonym of happy, and the two words are interchangeable. To say the stage and the dining-room are synonymous suggests that they are one and the same, and are thus likewise interchangeable

3. A centripetal motion is when things move towards the centre. A centrifugal motional, conversely, is when things move away from the centre.

4. To be subservient to someone means to be submissive or deferential to them.

5. The word "Marxian" refers to the nineteenth century philosopher, Karl Marx – the man responsible for dreaming up the idea of communism. To call a location a Marxian battleground is to suggest it's a location where communist-related conflicts play out.

ESSAY PLAN SIX

1. If a government is fiscally conservative, it means that they take the mentality that they should not spend too much money.

2. A symbiotic relationship is when both parties in that relationship feed off of the other.

3. To castigate someone is to sharply tell them off.

4. If you are proselytising, it means you are trying to convert someone to your way of thinking.

5. A soothsayer means something similar to a fortune teller: it is, in short, someone who is able to tell the future.

ESSAY PLAN SEVEN

1. In 1917, the Russian Bolshevik party – a communist party – instigated a seizure of power in Russia under the leadership of Vladimir Lenin. A civil war ensued, which the Bolsheviks ultimately won in 1922. This, unsurprisingly, sent political shockwaves through the entire world.

2. The phrase *et al.* is a Latin one, and it means 'and others.' Basically, it's a quicker to write "et al." than 'and Gerald'!

ESSAY PLAN EIGHT

1. The phrase sororal pride refers to sisterly pride.
2. An individual's self-conception is basically how they view themselves.
3. Another word for decorum might be etiquette. Decorum refers to the societal rules that people are expected to abide by.
4. To pay homage to someone is to acknowledge them in a respectful way, and usually in a way that indicates their superiority.
5. The denouement of a story/play is its final climax.

ESSAY PLAN NINE

1. A paradigm is a model way of doing things.
2. A polemic message is a message that argumentative and critical.

Printed in Great Britain
by Amazon